PRO SPORT CHAMP

NASCAR Sprir

Jennifer Howse

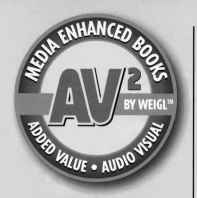

AV² provides enriched content that supplements and complements this book. Weigl's AV² books strive to create inspired learning and engage young minds in a total learning experience.

Your AV² Media Enhanced books come alive with...

Audio
Listen to sections of the book read aloud.

Key Words
Study vocabulary, and complete a matching word activity.

Video
Watch informative video clips.

Quizzes
Test your knowledge.

Embedded Weblinks
Gain additional information for research.

Slide Show
View images and captions, and prepare a presentation.

Try This!
Complete activities and hands-on experiments.

... and much, much more!

Go to **www.av2books.com,** and enter this book's unique code.

BOOK CODE

C689500

AV² **by Weigl** brings you media enhanced books that support active learning.

Published by AV² by Weigl
350 5ᵗʰ Avenue, 59ᵗʰ Floor
New York, NY 10118
Website: www.av2books.com   www.weigl.com

Library of Congress Cataloging-in-Publication Data
Howse, Jennifer.
 NASCAR Sprint Cup / Jennifer Howse.
    p. cm. -- (Pro sports championships)
 Includes index.
 ISBN 978-1-61913-616-8 (hardcover : alk. paper) -- ISBN 978-1-61913-618-2 (softcover : alk. paper)
 1. Stock car racing--United States--Juvenile literature. 2. Stock car drivers--United States--Juvenile literature. 3. NASCAR (Association)--Juvenile literature. I. Title.
 GV1029.9.S74H685 2013
 796.720973--dc23
                                         2012021767

Printed in the United States of America in North Mankato, Minnesota
1 2 3 4 5 6 7 8 9 16 15 14 13 12

062012
WEP170512

Project Coordinator Aaron Carr Design Terry Paulhus

CONTENTS

What is the NASCAR Sprint Cup?

The word **NASCAR** stands for National Association for Stock Car Auto Racing. NASCAR drivers compete in 36 races as part of the Sprint Cup Series each year. In the end, the driver who wins the most series races and collects the most points throughout the year wins the NASCAR Sprint Cup.

In a NASCAR race, 43 cars soar around a racetrack at speeds up to 200 miles (322 kilometers) per hour. These competitions pit **stock car** drivers against each other on different types of racetracks. Each race has cash prizes and a variety of off-track activities. Each driver is supported by a hard-working team of owners, crew members, and sponsors.

Tony Stewart won the 2011 NASCAR Sprint Cup Series Championship.

Since 1949, NASCAR racing has become one of the most popular sports in the United States. Millions of race fans gather at the track to watch these fast-paced events.

CHANGES THROUGHOUT THE YEARS

Past	Present
Regular cars with few changes to the body and engine were used in races.	Drivers race cars that are made up of specially designed parts.
Racing was done on oval, dirt tracks.	Today's tracks are carefully designed, **asphalt** courses.
Several races were held over a single weekend.	Qualifying races throughout the season lead up to one main race.
The racing series was called the Grand National.	The Sprint Cup Series is the top stock car racing championship.

Sprint Cup Trophy

Featuring a waving checkered flag, the Sprint Cup Trophy is the top prize in the Sprint Cup Series. The trophy is 24 inches (61 centimeters) tall and weighs 27 pounds (12 kilograms). Tiffany and Co. silversmiths created the Sprint Cup Trophy, which has a sterling silver top and a wooden base. The trophy is given to the winning driver, and two other trophies are awarded to the driver's team and sponsor. A Sprint Cup trophy is on permanent display at the Daytona 500 Experience, next to the Daytona International Speedway. This trophy has the names of all of the drivers who have won the cup engraved on it.

Sprint Cup History

At the turn of the 20th century, cars offered people a chance to move quickly from one place to another. As new car technology was developed, people began to gather and watch cars race.

Interest in stock car racing grew during the 1920s and early 1930s. People began making changes to their so cars they could travel faster. Over time, they began racing these **modified** cars in their free time.

Rex Mays won back-to-back national racing championships in 1940 and 1941.

In 1936, the first stock car race was held in Daytona Beach, Florida. Many people arrived early to watch the event, and the organizers had not yet arrived to take tickets. The race lost money for its organizers. As well, there were problems with the track. Another group decided to host the event the following year. Though the race was better organized, it still was not successful. Finally, a local stock car racer and mechanic, Bill France, and a restaurant owner named Charlie Reese took control of the event. They shared a small profit and held another event a month later. This time, they earned even more money. After that, France and Reese hosted several more races. Despite their early success, they were forced to put such events on hold during World War II.

The popularity of stock car racing grew during the 1920s and 1930s.

Richard Petty won the Winston Cup championship in 1974.

By the 1940s, stock car racing was a common pastime for many Americans. Across the country, a number of groups formed to cater to the fans and drivers of this sport. It became clear that a national organization was needed to bring these groups under a common set of rules.

Under France's guidance, the National Association for Stock Car Auto Racing (NASCAR) was formed in 1948. The first Grand National series was held in 1949. It included eight races on oval, dirt tracks, including the Daytona Beach Road course in Florida. The Grand National series grew quickly, eventually including up to 50 races.

In the 1960s, the series was reduced to 31 races per year. From 1971, the NASCAR series was called the Winston Cup.

In 1982, a new tradition was introduced to NASCAR races. From that time on, the first race of the series each year takes place at the Daytona International Raceway. Excitement builds for this annual event, and the series kicks off with great fanfare. In 2003, Nextel became the series sponsor, but after partnering with a company called Sprint, the series was renamed the Sprint Cup Series.

Sprint Cup Sponsors

An important part of a NASCAR team is the team's sponsor. Drivers and pit crews must earn an income. As well, stock cars are extremely expensive to maintain, fuel, and repair. Sponsors pay drivers to take part in races. They provide key funding in exchange for the opportunity to have the driver and car display their company **logos** and colors. Placement of these logos is important, and the top sponsor has the privilege of having its company logo on the hood of the car.

Rules of the Race

Since 1949, several rules have been established to ensure NASCAR races are fair and safe for drivers and **pit crews**. As new technology is developed, rules must be adjusted and updated. NASCAR **officials** conduct inspections of each car before the first practice, before and after qualifying races, as well as immediately before and after the main race. At the first race of the season at Daytona Speedway, a very thorough inspection is conducted to ensure cars are meeting guidelines for size, motors, and safety. This inspection sets a standard for the entire race season.

1 Car Engines

Engines are checked to see that they follow size guidelines and to ensure the **compression ratio** is correct. Most cars today have a fuel injection system that sprays gas directly into the engine. However, NASCAR vehicles must use a carburetor. This is a special device that mixes air and gas for the engine to burn as it runs. The power of the engine, or **horsepower**, can vary, but most race car engines are 750 to 790 horsepower.

2 Car Chassis

The chassis, or frame, of the car is made from fiberglass, a type of plastic that has glass fibers inside. It must be a specific size and shape. For example, the rear **spoiler** must be set at 70 degrees. The shape of the cars is based on designs by Ford, Chevrolet, Toyota, and Dodge. It can be changed slightly, but officials must check that the changes follow the rules. Roll bars also are an important part of the car chassis. They are a type of cage that protects the driver if a rollover occurs.

3 Car Mechanics

Stock car tires are a standard size and must be completely smooth, with no **treads**. A special gas tank, or fuel cell, gives all the cars about the same gas mileage. The fuel cells should contain no more than 22 gallons (83.2 liters) of fuel, as this affects the speed and durability of the car. They must be lined by foam rubber to prevent leaks.

5 Safety Checks

Safety belts, harnesses, and window nets are inspected to be sure they meet code. There are five belts that cross over the drivers to hold them securely in place. However, these belts can snap open quickly in an emergency. Officials check the safety belts to be certain that the correct material was used in their construction. Window nets are used so that, in case of a crash, the driver does not fall through the window.

4 Metal Parts

All of the metal parts of the car must be made from steel and not a lighter weight material, such as titanium. Officials use a magnet as a way to test if the proper materials have been used in the **manufacture** of the car. Magnets are attracted to steel parts, so the official can hold a magnet over the car parts to determine if they are steel.

Making the Call

After a car has been inspected, officials decide if it is fit to take part in the race. If officials do not approve a car to race, they can ask the team to replace parts. If, after a second inspection, these parts are not suitable, the driver, team, or car owner may face penalties or elimination from the race.

Once the race has begun, there are no set rules for how drivers compete on the track. An unwritten code of conduct encourages drivers to treat each other with respect and courtesy. If drivers are risking the safety of others, they can be penalized.

The Racetrack

By the 1960s, dirt oval tracks were closed down or paved. The last dirt track race was held in 1970, in Raleigh, North Carolina. Since then, the series has been run on 22 racetracks. These tracks are different lengths. Oval tracks that are less than 1 mile (1.6 kilometers) long are called short tracks. An intermediate or speedway track is 1 to 2 miles (1 to 3.2 km) in length. The longest tracks, or superspeedways, are more than 2 miles (3.2 km) long.

The longest NASCAR races are about 200 laps. On most tracks, all of the turns are to the left. However, on a type of racetrack called a road course, there are both left and right turns.

Race car fans can get to meet the drivers a few hours before the start of races.

Track speeds range from 90 to 200 miles (240 to 320 km) per hour. Special features of the track can make it faster or slower to drive. If a racetrack has level, or flat, turns, it is a slower track. If the track has raised, or inclined, turns called **banking**, it is a faster track. Bristol Motor Speedway in Tennessee has the highest track banking, at a 36-degree angle. This lets drivers and cars turn quickly and sharply. During the 1980s, high speeds of more than 200 miles (320 km) per hour were common on some tracks, such as Daytona and Talladega. As a result, speed restriction measures were put into place.

Driving the Track

Drivers race their cars at extremely fast speeds. Competing on the track involves shifting gears properly and moving the car around other cars to gain an advantage. Drivers often race in packs of three cars across a narrow stretch of track. Drivers in the packs that are leading the race do not want drivers from behind to pass them. The best time to pass is during a turn. Drivers behind other cars will stay very close to a leading car's **bumper**, waiting for a chance to move ahead. Tapping the front car on the bumper is a tactic used to move that car out of the way. If the lead drivers are much faster than the other cars in a race, they lap the slower cars on the track. This means that they have circled the track at least one full lap more than some of the slower drivers.

Talladega Superspeedway

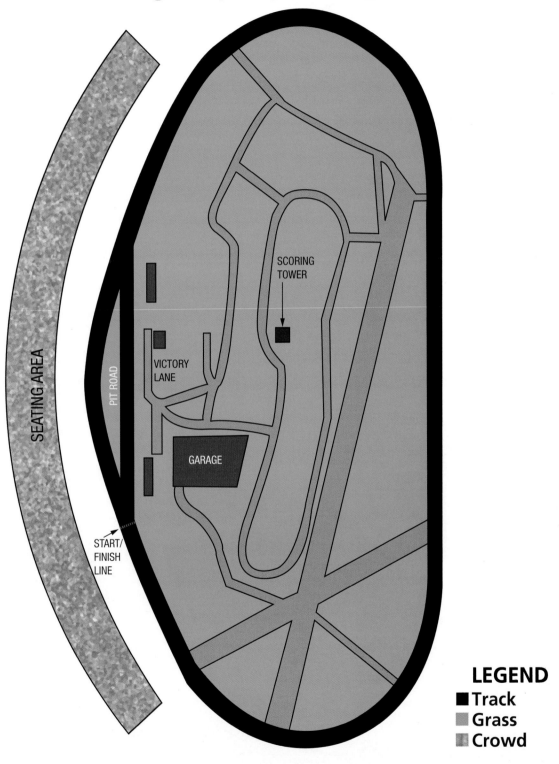

SEATING AREA

PIT ROAD

SCORING
TOWER

VICTORY
LANE

GARAGE

START/
FINISH
LINE

LEGEND
- ■ Track
- ■ Grass
- ▦ Crowd

Built for Speed

From the stands of a superspeedway, the crowd can hear the loud roar of the stock car engines as they speed around the track. Though they look like normal street cars, each of these race cars is specially designed for NASCAR. Engineers, physicists, mechanics, chemists, and car technology specialists all help to make NASCAR vehicles.

The first stock cars were bulky and heavy. Today, cars are sleek and **aerodynamic** so that they safely withstand great speeds. Each car weighs 3,400 pounds (1,542 kg), with a **wheelbase** of 110 inches (2.79 meters). Although the cars are made by different teams, there are some features that all stock cars must include, such as an eight-cylinder motor that is 358 cubic inches (5,867 cubic cm) in size.

When building a stock car, the hood, roof, and trunk are standard parts, but the rest of the car is custommade. This process involves shaping, pushing, pulling, forming, welding, and sealing the car.

Rollbar

Inside View

Decals/

Engine

Helmet

Fire-resistant suit

Shoes

Once completed, paint is applied for a glossy finish, and decals are stuck onto the car. Sponsor logos are added as a final touch.

Inside, the car is light in color, except for the red fuel line pipe. It is brightly colored so it can be found quickly if there is an emergency.

To enter a stock car, drivers must climb in through the window because the doors do not open.

There are three pedals on the floor—a gas pedal, a brake pedal, and a **clutch** pedal. The steering wheel is very tight and difficult to turn from right to left. This stiffness prevents the driver from turning too far if the car fishtails. Fishtailing is when the back of the car moves back and forth quickly.

Safety First

NASCAR drivers are racing professionals. They work hard to learn the skills needed to drive cars at high speeds. They also use special equipment to help keep them safe. Drivers wear a fire-resistant, one-piece suit. The suit must let the driver move easily enough to steer and climb out of the car quickly in the case of an emergency. Drivers wear helmets that are fitted with special monitors to ensure they do not breathe in harmful fumes from the engine. Seatbelts are made from tightly woven fabrics that do not stretch as much as those found in passenger cars. The seatbelts are fitted to each driver.

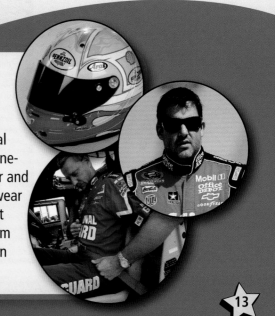

Chase for the Cup

By the end of the 2003 NASCAR season, Matt Kenseth had more points than any of the other racers. It was known that he would win the Sprint Cup even before the last races took place. As a result, people lost interest in watching those races. To prevent this from happening again, a new playoff point system was developed for the following season.

The Sprint Cup series is divided into two parts. After the first 26 races, the points and wins that each driver has earned to date are reviewed. The top 12 racers qualify for the playoffs, or the Chase for the Cup.

Drivers who qualify for the "Chase" are given extra points so that drivers outside of the top 12 will not be able to beat their final score. This point system guarantees the Sprint Cup winner will be one of the top 12 drivers. However, due to the extra points awarded to those drivers, the winner will not be determined until the last race, and sometimes, the last lap.

NASCAR organizers want all drivers to race competitively to the end of the season, even if they are not in the top 12 point scorers.

It is a tradition for the winner of a NASCAR race to spray his or her team with champagne.

The winner of a race is shown a checkered flag and crosses a checkered finish line.

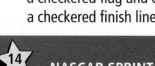

ony Stewart won the 2011 Sprint Cup in the final race of the Chase for the Cup.

o encourage this to happen, racers who do not qualify for the Chase
ave chances to win other awards. For example, throughout the season,
he winning driver of each race will receive a cash prize. During the final
hampionship event, the highest-ranking driver that is not a part of the
Chase wins a bonus of about one million dollars in prize money, among
ther honors.

Governing Body

NASCAR Research and Development is the governing body
for the safety of the sport. It is responsible for keeping
the sport competitive, as well as keeping the costs of
competing under control. Crashes sometimes occur, so
NASCAR Research and Development puts safety measures
in place to help prevent drivers from being injured. It tests
prototype cars by crashing them into walls at different angles.
As well, the cars are set on fire, pushed, pulled, and dragged to test the strength
and durability of the body, tires, engine, and safety equipment. All parts of the race
including, the track, are built for safety. Barriers along the race track walls are made
from a webbing of steel tubes that are filled and covered with rubber to absorb impacts.

Race Week

NASCAR sometimes impounds a car if it does not pass the pre-race inspection or meet specific criteria.

Several activities that lead up to the main event take place the week prior to a NASCAR race. On Monday, the teams check that all of their gear arrives and is ready for the race. Drivers have the day off.

Tuesday and Wednesday are days to test the cars. Drivers take the cars out onto the track to learn how to adjust the vehicles so they ride well on that specific course. The crew make changes to the car. On Thursday, drivers complete practice runs and work with the teams to get the cars ready for the qualifying events.

On Friday, drivers take part in qualifying races for one of the 35 spots in the final event. Another seven spots are open to drivers who may not have had a fast time but have enough points to qualify. A final spot is reserved for a past winner of the Sprint Cup who would not qualify otherwise. Drivers complete one or two laps around an empty track, driving as fast as possible. Drivers with the best times qualify to race in the final event. Their qualifying time determines the starting position in the final race. Drivers spend Saturday practicing on the track, trying to improve their times. Final adjustments are made to the cars.

Race day is Sunday, and the main event begins with the sponsor's meeting. Race fans get a chance to meet the drivers and ask questions. After the sponsor's meeting, the drivers meet for two hours to discuss rule changes and the conditions of the track.

Before drivers get into their cars, they wave to the crowds and walk across the track. The national anthem is played, and a tribute to the military is performed as jets fly over the racetrack. Once the drivers have been strapped into the cars, an announcement is made to tell the drivers to start their cars.

At first, cars do warmup laps to help them establish their speed. Before the actual race begins, all of the moving cars line up in position behind the **pace car**. The race begins when a green flag is waved. A checkered flag is dropped as the winning car and driver cross the finish line. After the race, there is a big celebration in the winner's circle, and the trophy is handed to the winning team.

The race cars form a pace line at the start of a race.

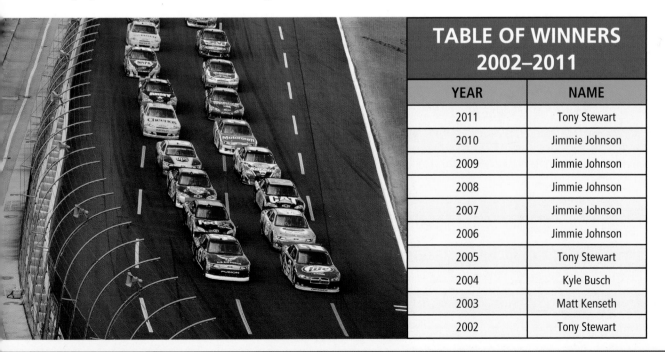

TABLE OF WINNERS 2002–2011	
YEAR	NAME
2011	Tony Stewart
2010	Jimmie Johnson
2009	Jimmie Johnson
2008	Jimmie Johnson
2007	Jimmie Johnson
2006	Jimmie Johnson
2005	Tony Stewart
2004	Kyle Busch
2003	Matt Kenseth
2002	Tony Stewart

Mapping NASCAR Tracks

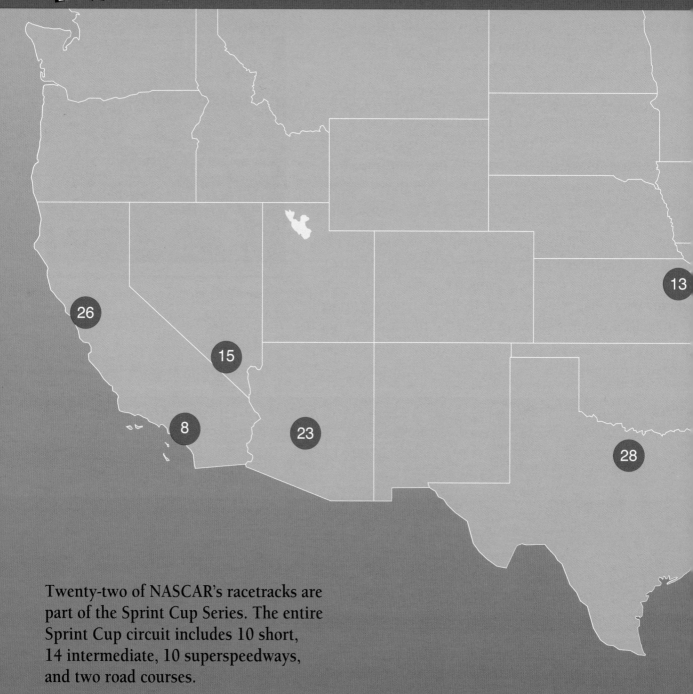

Twenty-two of NASCAR's racetracks are part of the Sprint Cup Series. The entire Sprint Cup circuit includes 10 short, 14 intermediate, 10 superspeedways, and two road courses.

LEGEND

● NASCAR tracks across the United States

N
W · E
S

Scale ___ 621 Miles
0 ___ 1,000 Kilometers

POCONO

NASCAR TRACKS

1) Atlanta Motor Speedway
2) Bristol Motor Speedway
3) Charlotte Motor Speedway
4) Chicagoland Speedway
5) Darlington Raceway
6) Daytona International Speedway
7) Dover International Speedway
8) Auto Club Speedway
9) Homestead-Miami Speedway
10) Indianapolis Motor Speedway
11) Lucas Oil Raceway
12) Iowa Speedway
13) Kansas Speedway
14) Kentucky Speedway
15) Las Vegas Motor Speedway
16) Martinsville Speedway
17) Memphis Motorsports Park
18) Michigan International Speedway
19) The Milwaukee Mile
20) Nashville Superspeedway
21) New Hampshire Motor Speedway
22) Phoenix International Raceway
23) Pocono Raceway
24) Richmond International Raceway
25) Infineon Raceway
26) Talladega Superspeedway
27) Texas Motor Speedway
28) Watkins Glen International

Women and Racing

Although most NASCAR drivers are men, women sometimes take part in the sport as well.

In 1977, Janet Guthrie qualified to start at the Daytona 500. She was the first woman to earn a spot in the cup series. In the same season, Guthrie raced in the **Indy 500**. The following year, Guthrie finished ninth at the Indy 500 and won $84,000. Guthrie had her best finish at the Milwaukee 200, taking fifth place. She built her own team and paved the way for other women to take part in car racing events. In 2006, Guthrie was inducted into the International Motorsports Hall of Fame.

Tammy Jo Kirk began competing in the NASCAR truck series in 1997. She paved the way for women to take part in stock car racing.

In 1991, Tammy Jo Kirk became the first female driver to race in the Slim Jim All Pro Series. She also won the end of the season Snowball Derby at Five Flags Speedway in Pensacola, Florida. Kirk was the first woman to win two Busch Pole Awards in the 1996 series. She was chosen as the most popular driver and made headway for women in stock car racing. In 1997, Kirk began competing in the NASCAR truck series, winning $134,000 in prize money. She finished seventh of 29 rookies. Kirk also competes in motocross races.

Janet Guthrie raced in the 1977 Winston Cup Daytona 500.

At the age of 16, Patty Moise began racing in the International Motor Sport Association (IMSA) series. By 1986, Moise had entered her first **Busch Series** race and was the first woman to lead a Busch series race. Her last Busch Series season was in 1998, when she took part in 19 races.

Louise Smith raced in many kinds of vehicles from 1949 to 1956. She drove in the Grand Nationals and had a third-place finish at the Greenville-Pickens Speedway in South Carolina. Throughout her career, Smith won 38 races. In the 1970s, Smith returned to the racing world as a sponsor.

In 2010, Danica Patrick joined the NASCAR Nationwide Series. Patrick is the only woman in history to win an IndyCar series race. She also finished third in an Indianapolis 500, the highest finish ever by a woman. Her switch to the NASCAR circuit brought many new fans to stock car racing.

Danica Patrick won the 2008 Indy Japan 300.

Women in the Pits

In 2006, Nicole Addison was the first woman to join a pit crew team. A mechanic and tire specialist, Nicole trained hard for her position as a rear tire changer. Nicole participated in PIT Instruction and Training, which involves eight weeks of physical training, drills, and trials. She worked and practiced until she felt she was good enough to earn her place and make a positive contribution to her team. Nicole's shop duties include installing decals on trucks, ensuring the tires are ready for each race, and making sure there are tires ready for testing the tracks. She enjoys the fast-paced truck series and helping her race team win.

Historical Highlights

Stock car racing is a very dangerous sport. Over the years, NASCAR races have had many terrible crashes. Officials try to learn from crashes to improve safety and prevent future accidents. On May 24, 1964, Glen Roberts was racing at the Charlotte Motor Speedway when he swerved to avoid a crash and hit a gate. In an instant, Roberts' car flipped and caught fire. Roberts died from his injuries. After the crash, NASCAR officials changed the rules so that all fuel cells were rubber lined and almost impossible to puncture.

In 1960, CBS Sports broadcast its first live NASCAR Grand National Division event called the "CBS Sports Spectacular." For the first time, television viewers were able to see the Grand National Pole Position races from Daytona. Announcer Bud Palmer hosted the two-hour program that was the first devoted entirely to stock car racing.

NASCAR races were first broadcast on the radio in 1970. People tuned in to racing, but the broadcasts also made stars of the drivers. By 1983, TV coverage cameras were mounted inside the cars to bring viewers right into the action.

Crashes in stock car races have resulted in new rules and safety procedures.

n 1967, Mario Andretti competed in several different series, including the NASCAR Grand National Division. In only his second run at the Daytona 500, he won, making history. Andretti is a legendary and extremely skillful racing driver who holds many records and has earned several racing accomplishments.

n 1988, Bobby Allison and his son finished irst and second at the Daytona 500 race. This incredible finish for the Allison family highlights how generations of drivers have defined he sport.

n 1998, NASCAR celebrated its 50th anniversary. As part of the celebrations, Las Vegas Motor Speedway was added to the season schedule. Mark Martin won the inaugural event at this speedway on March 1, 1998.

In 1988, Bobby Allison won the Daytona 500, and his son Davey finished second.

n 2010, Jimmie Johnson set a record by winning his fifth consecutive Sprint Cup. That year, he finished the regular season with six wins and 23 finishes in the top 10.

NASCAR RECORDS

RECORD	DRIVER
Most Sprint Cup Championship Wins – 7	Richard Petty and Dale Earnhardt
Youngest Sprint Cup Winner – 23 years	Bill Rexford
Oldest Sprint Cup Winner – 45 years	Bobby Allison
Biggest Lead at a NASCAR Race Finish Line – 14 laps	Ned Jarrett
Closest NASCAR Finishes – 0.002 seconds	Ricky Craven over Kurt Busch, Jimmie Johnson over Clint Bowyer

LEGENDS
and Current Stars

Jeff Gordon

In 1992, Jeff Gordon raced for the first time in the cup series. Over his career, he has had many major wins. He was only the second driver ever to win the Winston Million. A winner of four cup series championships, Gordon has a total of 85 cup series wins. Gordon won the South 500s four times in a row. In 1995 and 1997, Gordon was named Driver of the Year.

Richard Petty

Jeff Gordon

Richard Petty

With several series cup wins over his 35-year career, Richard Petty is thought to be the king of the stock car racing circuit. In the 1967 season, Petty won 41 out of 48 races. Of the 12,739 laps Petty raced, he led 5,537. Petty is the number one NASCAR driver in history, with 200 all-time wins and 555 top-five finishes. He retired in 1992 and was inducted into the Lowe's Motor Speedway Court of Legends. Petty was inducted into the NASCAR Hall of Fame in 2010.

Jimmie Johnson

Dale Earnhardt

From his first season in the NASCAR cup series, Dale Earnhardt was a winning driver. He had a total of 76 wins, which earned him $41,538,362. Earnhardt was the all-time winner at the Daytona International Speedway, and he won the National Motorsport Press Association's Driver of the Year Award five times. In 2001, Earnhardt died in a crash during the last lap of the Daytona 500.

Jimmie Johnson

From 2006 to 2010, Jimmie Johnson won five series cup championships in a row. No other driver has won more than three in a row. Johnson is eighth on the list of all-time series championship drivers, with more than 50 wins. Starting out driving in the Busch Series, Johnson made his break into the series cup in 2002. He finished fifth as a rookie. Johnson is the only racing driver to be named Associated Press Male Athlete of the Year.

Dale Earnhardt

Famous Firsts

Since the first meeting of the NASCAR founders, stock car racing has become a major international sport. The first Daytona 500 was raced on February 22, 1959. Speeds reached 140 miles (225 km) per hour. The race was won by Lee Petty. This started a long tradition of holding the top racing events in Florida. The high-banked 2.5-mile (4-km) Daytona International Speedway hosted the first Daytona 500. More than 41,000 fans attended the inaugural event. The winner was decided 61 hours after the checkered flag flew.

On September 4, 1950, the Southern 500, NASCAR's first 500-mile race, was held at Darlington Raceway in South Carolina. Johnny Mantz won the race in an exciting finish.

On December 1, 1963, Wendell Scott became the first African American driver to win a race in the Grand National Series, which is now the Sprint Cup. He remains the only African American driver to have won in the series. He began his racing career driving homebuilt modified cars in 1954. He was the first full-time African American driver to run the NASCAR circuit. In 1959, at the age of 38, Scott won the Virginia State Sportsman championship. Two years later, he took part in the Grand National Series. In nearly 500 Grand National races, he was in the top 10 147 times. Scott's driving career ended in 1973, when he sustained three cracked ribs, a lacerated arm, and a cracked pelvis in a 21-car pileup at the Talladega Superspeedway.

In 1959, Lee Petty won the first Daytona 500.

Wendell Scott was the first full-time African American driver to compete in the NASCAR circuit.

In March 2008, for the first time in 54 years of racing history, a non-American built car won a NASCAR race. Toyota car number 18 was driven by Kyle Busch during a race at the Las Vegas Motor Speedway. That same month, Kyle captured the coveted first place finish at the Kobalt Tools 500 in Atlanta. He was the youngest driver to win in Atlanta.

In 2011, for the first time in cup history, the championship was determined by a tie breaker. Both Tony Stewart and Carl Edwards had the same number of points after the final race. However, Stewart had more wins during the regular season, so the championship was awarded to him.

In 2008, Kyle Busch became the first driver to win a NASCAR race in a non-American made car. He drove a Toyota, a car built in Japan.

NASCAR Championship Leagues

In 1952, NASCAR became an international sport by hosting a race in Canada. The National Championship series, which is now known as the Sprint Cup, included a race on a 0.5-mile (0.8-km) dirt oval, called Stamford Park, in Ontario, Canada. A few years later, another race was run at the Canadian Exposition Stadium in Toronto. The races were a success, and NASCAR decided to hold exhibition races in Japan. The first race at Suzuka was won by Rusty Wallace. In 1997, a second race at Suzuka was won by Mike Skinner. The third race, in 1998, was won by Skinner at Japan's new 1.5-mile (2.4-km) oval at Twin Ring Motegi. Today, new championship leagues have opened up, and NASCAR holds more than 1,500 races each year.

The Rise of the Sprint Cup

1947

Led by Bill France, a strictly stock car racing league is formed at Daytona Beach, Florida. Within a year, the first official NASCAR race is held on the Daytona Beach Road Course.

1959

The first Daytona 500 takes place at a new racetrack that will serve as the world center of stock car racing.

1964

Richard Petty wins the Daytona 500, driving at speeds higher than 175 miles (282 km) per hour.

1967

Mario Andretti races a Ford car at the Daytona 500.

1969

The first NASCAR race at Talladega Superspeedway takes place. Drivers reach practice speeds of 200 miles (322 km) per hour.

1971

The Grand National Cup becomes the Winston Cup. The series bonus prize money increases by $100,000.

1978

Dale Earnhardt debuts at the Charlotte Motor Speedway as a last minute replacement. Two years later, he wins the series championship.

1979

One race in the series is shown on television. Within 10 years, all NASCAR series races are broadcast.

1985

Bill Elliot sets the speed record at the Talladega Superspeedway at 205 miles (330 km) per hour.

1987

Bobby Allison crashes his car. It launches into the air and lands in the stands. After the crash, new rules are put in place.

1994

Dale Earnhardt matches Richard Petty's championship record by winning his seventh Sprint Cup.

2001

A crash ends the life of racing legend Dale Earnhardt in the final lap of the Daytona 500.

2009

Jimmie Johnson wins his fourth Sprint Cup championship.

2011

Tony Stewart wins his first Sprint Cup title, ending Jimmie Johnson's record streak of five championships in a row.

QUICK FACTS

- The windshield in a stock car is made of a tough material called Lexan. Lexan scratches easily, so layers of plastic are smoothed over the top of the glass. Throughout the race, layers of plastic are removed. This gives the driver a new view without dust or scratches.

- Drivers do not know what speed their car is going. There are no speedometers in a stock car.

- Temperatures inside the cockpit can reach 140° Fahrenheit (60° Celsius).

Test Your Knowledge

1 When was the Chase for the Cup format added to the Sprint Cup?

2 Why did NASCAR change the point system and create the Chase for the Cup?

3 When were NASCAR races first broadcast on radio?

4 Name two pieces of safety equipment that can save a driver in an emergency.

5 Where is the first race held to start the Sprint Cup series each year?

6 Who was the first woman driver to compete in the Sprint Cup Series?

7 Who was the first woman to join a pit crew team?

8 What two countries other than the United States also have NASCAR events?

9 Who was the first African American NASCAR driver?

10 Who won the first Daytona 500?

ANSWERS: 1) 2004 2) NASCAR wanted to make all of the races more competitive. 3) 1970 4) Seatbelts, netting, helmet, or fire resistant suit 5) The Daytona International Speedway 6) Janet Guthrie in 1977 7) Nicole Addison 8) Canada and Japan 9) Wendell Scott 10) Lee Petty

Key Words

aerodynamic: shaped to move fast through the air

asphalt: humanmade surface of a racetrack

banking: sloping roadway

bumper: front and back protection on a car

Busch Series: a series of races for less-experienced drivers who want to prove they can race in the Sprint Cup

clutch: a pedal that disconnects the engine from the transmission

compression ratio: a number that is used to predict how well an engine will perform

horsepower: the power of an engine

Indy 500: a 500-mile race held on Memorial Day weekend each year at the Indianapolis Motor Speedway in Indiana

logos: signs that have a company name and colors

manufacture: to build a car

modified: changed from its original state

NASCAR: National Association for Car Auto Racing; the largest governing body of stock car racing

officials: people who are in charge of how a race is run

pace car: a car that sets the position of the cars on the track and the pace for the race

pit crews: people who work in an area on the side of a race track where cars are serviced

prototype cars: cars built for safety testing but not for racing

spoiler: a flap on a car that keeps it from being lifted off the road when traveling at high speeds

stock car: street car that is specially designed for racing

treads: patterns on a tire which give the tire grip

wheelbase: the distance between the front and back wheels on a car

Index

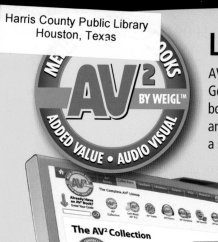

Log on to www.av2books.com

AV[2] by Weigl brings you media enhanced books that support active learning. Go to www.av2books.com, and enter the special code found on page 2 of this book. You will gain access to enriched and enhanced content that supplements and complements this book. Content includes video, audio, web links, quizzes, a slide show, and activities.

Audio
Listen to sections of the book read aloud.

Video
Watch informative video clips.

Embedded Weblinks
Gain additional information for research.

Try This!
Complete activities and hands-on experiments.

WHAT'S ONLINE?

Try This!	Embedded Weblinks	Video	EXTRA FEATURES
Try a stock car racing activity.	Learn more about the NASCAR Sprint Cup.	Watch a video about the NASCAR Sprint Cup.	**Audio** Listen to sections of the book read aloud.
Test your knowledge of NASCAR equipment.	Read about legendary NASCAR drivers through history.	Watch a video about star NASCAR drivers.	**Key Words** Study vocabulary, and complete a matching word activity.
Label the features of a NASCAR racetrack.	Find out more about the drivers that have won the most NASCAR Sprint Cup championships.		**Slide Show** View images and captions, and prepare a presentation.
Complete a timeline activity.			**Quizzes** Test your knowledge.

AV[2] was built to bridge the gap between print and digital. We encourage you to tell us what you like and what you want to see in the future.

Sign up to be an AV[2] Ambassador at www.av2books.com/ambassador.

Due to the dynamic nature of the Internet, some of the URLs and activities provided as part of AV[2] by Weigl may have changed or ceased to exist. AV[2] by Weigl accepts no responsibility for any such changes. All media enhanced books are regularly monitored to update addresses and sites in a timely manner. Contact AV[2] by Weigl at 1-866-649-3445 or av2books@weigl.com with any questions, comments, or feedback.